Cover design by Law Cheuk Yui / cheukyui.com
Book design by Law Cheuk Yui

Michael Andrew Law
Visit my website at www.michaelandrewlaw.com

First Printing: 2015
Shop Cheuk Yui

Michael Andrew Law
Artist Statement
「藝術家自述」

My paintings tries to captured the Soul of Youth , I combines classical mediums such as Pigment & Oil with contemporary painting method and medium such as Digital CG as Giclée Prints , I Only interested on ONE but immortal subject matters : Female Figures, by set against the figures with chinese calligraphy Employing the Idea of Word as Image, as an expressive scenario . I use both Life models and Computer Generated Images for the creation of works .

Through juxtaposition, both Icons (The Words and Female figures) , Both added meanings to the other.

These paintings are My Own interpret and to document HongKong's own Millennial and its Generation's view point and identities : As "Hongkonger".

oil on canvas 30x30"

oil on canvas 32x46"

oil on canvas 9x4'

Michael Andrew Law at Work.

Michael Andrew Law

Michael Andrew Law (Born Law Cheuk Yui) was born 1982 in British Hong Kong. After studying Classical oil painting private lessons with New York Artist Daniel Anderson (1928 - 2008) at the his then-new workshop in Hong Kong, he made a stunning reputation as the designer of a number of cover spreads for the press in Hong Kong and abroad and as an illustrator and creative designer of various Comic Books / Story Books .

He then stepped away from commercial work and devoted himself solely to Oil painting. In recent years, he has aesthetically moved away from a stylistic "Icons Photorealist" to HongKonger-Realism, pushing his rendered subjects into a mythological arena. His artistic visions are treasured and collected by many . From there, Law quickly gained recognition in the art world by exhibiting at Hong Kong Convention and Exhibition Centre , The Avenue of Stars ; Law´s works are also appreciated and collected by many Hong Kong and international collectors.

Some of Law's Religious artworks for Catholic Church of Hong Kong are also gained media attention in 2006 and 2007 ,and was also received by the Cardinal of the Catholic Church in the same year .

His Pale Hair Girls are a thoroughly subversive tribute to the world of appearances worshipers and to the Hong Kong's Millennial Generation culture of 21 century, with which the painter has cultivated an almost ritualistic relationship. His paintings provoke and compel. There is a unique realness in spirit.

The artist lives and works at Central District , Hong Kong.

Solo Show at NatureArt Gallery

At Ceremony with the Cardinal

Michael Andrew Law

(852) 6444-7550
info@michaelandrewlaw.com
www.michaelandrewlaw.com

HONORS AND AWARDS:

*Medici Cast Study Recognized by Social Fine Arts Grade Examination Center Of China Academy Of Art.
*Social Fine Arts Grade Examination Center Of China Academy Of Art Promotional Art(2011-present)
Publishers Weekly Best illustrated 's Coffe Book 2004 (Pete M.Parks)
The Salt and The Light Catholic Church Children Book 2004 (Mars)
Borders Magazine Most Original Voices nominee 2006 (Dear Fish)
Publisher's Weekly Best Children's Book list 2004 (America the Beautiful)
Communication Digital Artist -- Award of Excellence
European Print Weekly Design Annual Awards (2000,2002)
Face to face Dolphin art competition silver award 2006
Art Directors of HKC Award of Merit (2005)
Society of Fine Art -- An exhibitor 2005 Society of Newspaper Design Award of Excellence
Michael and Stephanie Duo Exhibition (2006)
Spectrum Fantastic Art Annual (multiple)
not-for-profit aution for Rotary of HK 2012

Art Funtion for Organic Beauty opening

Exhibition :

2013 DeTour Matters 2013 Satellite Events at NatureArt Gallery
2013 December to Remember , One man show at NatureArt Gallery Central District, Hong Kong.
2012 Solo Show , Park Central tseung kwan O ,Hong Kong
2011 Art Walk Group Showing , Discovery Bay ,Hong Kong
2011 HK Gold Coast (Book signing exhibition)
2009 Solo Painting Exhibition The Avenue of Stars
Group Exhibition of Daniel Anderson workshop Classical Realism class of 2008 at Manhattan,NY
2007 Guest and ExhibitionThe Peak Galleria Hong Kong
2007 Invited workshop exhibition, Elements, Hong Kong
Group Exhibition of Classical Realism class of 2007 at Manhattan,NY
2006 Collection by Cardinal Zen Ze-kiun and exhibited at Catholic Church of Hong Kong.
2004 - 2007, Hong Kong Young Artist Group Exhibition, Hong Kong Central Library.
Group Exhibition of Classical Realism class of 2006 at East Village, Manhattan,NY
2005 Illustration original exhibition for Kung Kao Po
2004 Group Exhibition, Wanchai Tower
2003 Group Exhibition, Hong Kong Convention and Exhibition Centre.
2003 Winner of I luv Hong Kong Painting Competition, exhibition at The Landmark (Hong Kong).
2002 The Holy story Picture Book illustrated picture original exhibition ,sai wan ho civic centre.

Art Funtion at The Peninsula Hong Kong

SELECTED COLLECTIONS :

Cardinal of the Catholic Church Joseph Zen Ze-kiun
Organic Beauty Inc
Agriculture, Fisheries and Conservation Department
Ms.Ho Wei Ying
Ms. Annie Yu
Daniel Anderson
MR.Tsang Yan Sam

Interview with Hollywood Film Producer / Teacher Dov Simens

PUBLICATIONS :

Fisheye magazine , featured artist interview , November 2002 (ISBN: N/A)
Kung Kao Po , interview , June 2006 (ISBN: N/A)
Art of Rock Realism , 2008 (ISBN: N/A)
Michael Andrew Law Early works Volume 1 - 3 :
(ISBN-13: 978-1503319400)
(ISBN-13: 978-1503366060)
(ISBN-13: 978-1503365087)
The Pale Hair Girls of Michael Andrew Law , 2010 (ISBN-13: 9781503372115)
December to Remember One man Show Art Book , 2013 (ISBN-13: 9781505609257)
Christmas Everyday : Pale Hair Girls Christmas Series 1 (ISBN-13: 978-1505453218)
Christmas Everyday : Pale Hair Girls Christmas Series 2 (ISBN-13: 978-1505467796)
Christmas Everyday : Pale Hair Girls Christmas Series 3 (ISBN-13: 978-1505468052)
Christmas Everyday : Pale Hair Girls Christmas Series 4 (ISBN-13: 978-1505470741)
Christmas Everyday : Pale Hair Girls Christmas Series 5 (ISBN-13: 978-1505470857)
Christmas Everyday : Pale Hair Girls Christmas Series 6 (ISBN-13: 978-1505471151)
Christmas Everyday : Pale Hair Girls Christmas Series Specials (ISBN-13: 978-1505583922)
i-Egoism by Michael Andrew Law (ISBN:978-1-4990-2124-0)

Exhibition at Hong Kong Central Library.

Group Exhibition at Hong Kong Museum of Art

Exhibition at Avenue of Stars, Hong Kong (2010)

Exhibition at Hong Kong Convention and Exhibition Centre.

關 於藝術家MICHAEL ANDREW LAW:

生長於交接時期香港的年輕藝術家 Michael Andrew Law，擅長把數碼繪圖，Pop 摩登藝術及古典油畫揉合時事及諷刺，創出獨特的視覺藝術語言及內容，跨越中西混合背景思維界限，探索互聯網世代交錯回歸的中西混雜之香港歷史。

他以自由隨意的手法結合摩登及古典材料與技巧，保持表現與認知、控制與隨性、魯妄與機智、自我與社羣等對立美學力量之間的張力，並對香港Y世代、本土文化及民族社會的殘酷現實作出尖刻的評論。Michael Andrew Law 的作品色彩豐富，寫實風格描繪的冰山美人，刻畫在滿佈流行文化圖像、東方書法標誌及符號的背景上。《白髮女孩糸列》(The Pale Hair Girls，2006 — 2013 年) 的創作之中，Michael Andrew Law 獨特的繪畫風格呈獻出達達主義思考方式般的且出人意表的效果。畫中冰山美人式的人物穿插在抽象的香港和俗世符號上。

Pale Hair Girls糸列的畫作的視覺靈感大量源自法國美術學院派大師William-Adolphe Bouguereau 的少年油畫作品以及已故華裔畫家陳逸飛的史詩及美人作品，Michael Andrew Law一反傳統的繪畫技法，以數碼混合古典繪畫技，重新演繹細緻複雜的中西方古典畫面和精心纖細思考的構圖，以西式媒介呼應中國的傳統書法裡作為圖案之筆觸，在 Michael Andrew Law 的筆下這種交錯西式POP ART和中式古典藝術表現時輪廓卻非常細緻，尤其最廣為流傳和臨摹的Leonardo da Vinci作品Mona Lisa (1517 年)，以東方血統之妻子肖像取代現代Mona Lisa 的表徵意義，極具質感的厚顏料同時呈現寫生畫作時人物肉體的細微變化。

《誰會理會不是自己的新天地:三聯畫》(Humanity) 刻畫了在世代末日的未來世代們於本為廢墟的香港島上，等待著他們的命運。這些離奇的場景與Jerry B. Jenkins及Timothy LaHaye等當代作家描寫的超現實、宗教解讀、未來主義情懷如出一致。於半島酒店扶輪會演講當代藝術

主要探索他藝術裡其中一項最重要的二分法：浪漫與嘲諷、作為藝術家對美的浪漫思考及交匯中西混合背景思維之香港Y世代的悲情，由天真燦爛的冰山美人式少女與可怕的末日和俗物之間的強烈對比作象徵。無論是標誌性的單幅「古典書法圖案的無身份肖像」，抑或以三聯畫形式出現，運用到大師級繪畫與構圖技巧，揉合了精細傳統油畫技法與摩登的表現方式建構，美人亦在美術史和流行文化裡是永恆的主題。冰山美人式少女令人聯想到生命的脆弱與時光飛逝之無情。藝術家就是要了解不同世界之間的界線並翻譯到不同文化價值之間的語境如高尚對低俗、古代對現代、東方對西方。

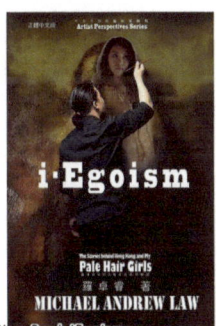

New Book iEgoism
ISBN:978-1-4990-2124-0

憑著 iEgoism 故事性的風格和精神，Michael Andrew Law將流行、古典與時事內容混合成一種感覺超豐富的視覺藝術作品，所涉獵的美學領域和文化靈感不斷延伸，而他在當中游走自如。一如常見的當代藝術主題，去作為「諷刺」及「反思」有關「浪漫」與「悲情」的直接敘述。

他所開發的iEgoism主題，就深受當代或反傳統藝術愛好者的喜愛，這被視為跟西方DADA藝術主義互相呼應。Michael Andrew Law把自己置身於他熱烈的自我網世代主義- iEgoism裡展現出的姿態卻是完全屬於他本人和他的時代的。

Michael Andrew Law於2006 年隨美國紐約藝術家Daniel Anderson深造古典油畫，其後發展純美術繪畫工作，2008年獲贊助於香港中環成立藝術工作室 Nature Art。除了製作藝術及相關作品，Nature Art 及 Michael Andrew Law 亦積極培育香港年輕藝術家。

2013 年，他於NatureArt Gallery舉行藝術展覽《iEgoism》，從香港歷史中追溯當代香港流行視覺藝術文化的特徵。

Michael Andrew Law 的作品曾於紐約 Chelsea 的聯合展覽中展出，他亦曾在著名機構及學校舉行個展及講座，例如星光大道 (2009 年)、天主教香港教區、香港中央圖育館(2004 -2007 年)、灣仔政府大樓外(2004 年)，香港會議展覽中心 (2003 年)。2015出版藝術文字著作《不可不知的藝術家觀點系列-iEgoism》更深入探討香港Y世代、香港歷史和Michael Andrew Law的作品脈絡關聯。

Michael Andrew Law 現於香港定居及從事創作。

Michael Andrew Law fusing digital and classical painting with west and East creative philosophy , to produce an extremely original artistic language and content that bridged west and east ,classical and modern medium , at the same time clearly tells the stories of his own generation. Combining digital creative materials and classical painting techniques with effusive yet knowing and precise focused , his paintings maintain a powerful tension between opposing aesthetic forces—expression and knowledge, control and spontaneity, savagery and wit, urbanity and primitivism—while providing satiric commentary on the oppressive realities of the predicament of Generation Internet, homegrown hongkonger's local-culture vesus Traditional Chinese culture, and The Hong Kong's post-handover history.

In his dynamically designed compositions, gracefully detailed figures and innocent faces are incise against fields that juxtaposed with portraits, chinese calligraphy, and sometimes cgi. The Pale Hair Girls Series (2006 - 2013) depicts realistic cold, icy-like young female figures surrounded by abstract and expressively painted forms and shapes revealing images of Pop culture, Historial figures, and Hong Kong landmarks.

Michael Andrew Law draws inspiration from Old Master's works such as Caravaggio , Ruben , Rembrandt , all the way to the Modern Art Superstars such as Warhol , Lichtenstein , Richter , De Kooning , Bacon , Wool and Prince . The Pale Hair Girls series mainly inspired by the painting works of French academic painter and traditionalist William-Adolphe Bouguereau and the Late Great YiFei Chen's characteristic "Romantic Realism" paintings.

In a reversal of standard East-West aesthetics, Law re-interprets Old Master's sophisticated imagery combine classical and digital materials—which resonate with Digital Vector Designs and Paintings—with fine strokes of oil paint multi-layered with paint film.In his interpretation of Leonardo Da Vinci's iconic Mona Lisa's smile (1517)—an iconic image that has been endlessly disseminated and reproduced—Law painted over the symbolism of the portrait Mona Lisa with his young wife , intent on rendering the figure in contemporary fashion with the iconic image as background .

 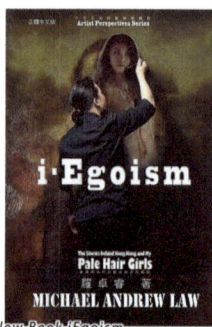

New Book 'iEgoism'
ISBN:978-1-4990-2124-0

"The Humanity triptych" depicts New Generation HongKongers in a Ruined Hong Kong city , awaiting their unknown fate of a new beginning. This painting series explores one of the central paradox of his art—between romance and derision , his romantic magnanimity as an artist and his pessimistic perspective on the predicament of Generation Y Hongkongers. Here, this paradox is symbolized by the stark contrast of icy cold young female and disturbing representations of the armageddon-like of images. Whether portrayed as single "chinese calligraphy " or in triptych composition and classical paintwork that combine both expressive and traditional painting techniques with the digital vector , the beauties and the human figures stand as eternal motifs in the history of art and also in popular culture. Both oppositional and parallel, they are reminders of the fragile vibrancy of life and the impitoyable passing of time.

A references between different cultural refrence (high/pop, classical/contemporary, east/west), Michael Andrew Law has stated that an artist should be someone who understood how to hybrid between different worlds and go ahead makes an effort to knowing them. With his distinctive "iEgoism" philosophy , which employs highly refined academic painting techniques to depict a mixture of abstract expressionism within a representational pop culture images. These techniques parallel to the themes of romance and predicament of this generation , he recollects and revitalizes narratives of irony and introspection.

Michael Andrew Lawwas born in 1982 in British Hong Kong , studied fine art with american artist Daniel Anderson and graduate of China Central Academy of Fine Arts Sam Zeng from 2003 - 2006 . He co-founded the Hong Kong Art Studio Nature Art Workshop in 2008. In addition to the production and marketing of Michael Andrew Law's art and related work, Nature Art functions as a supportive environment for the fostering of emerging Hong Konger artists. Law is also a curator. In 2013, he organized an exhibition of contemporary art titled "iEgoism ," which served as a narration of contemporary HongKong Gen Y pop culture .

Michael Andrew Law

(852) 6444-7550

info@michaelandrewlaw.com
www.michaelandrewlaw.com

Selected publications

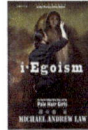

iEgoism by Michael Andrew Law
Softcover : 110 pages
Publisher : Xlibris LLC
ISBN: Softcover 978-1-4990-2124-0
ISBN: EBook 978-1-4990-2118-9

Michael Andrew Law The early years volume one: Nine Drawings from the early years collection
ISBN-10: 1503319407
ISBN-13: 978-1503319400

Michael Andrew Law The early years volume Two: Nine more Drawings from the early years collection (Volume 2)
ISBN-10: 1503365085
ISBN-13: 978-1503365087

Michael Andrew Law The early years volume Three: Nine Drawings from the early years collection (Volume 3)
ISBN-10: 1503366065
ISBN-13: 978-1503366060
Product Dimensions: 6 x 0.1 x 9 inches

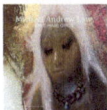

Michael Andrew Law: Pale Hair Girls Catalogue (Volume 1)
Paperback: 124 pages
ISBN-10: 1503372111
ISBN-13: 978-1503372115
Product Dimensions: 8.5 x 0.3 x 8.5 inches

 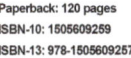

December To Remember: Michael Andrew Law Exhibition
Paperback: 120 pages
ISBN-10: 1505609259
ISBN-13: 978-1505609257

Hong Kong Artist Series: Michael Andrew Law 1
Paperback: 48 pages
ISBN-10: 1507580665
ISBN-13: 978-1507580660

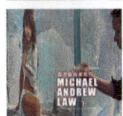

Hong Kong Artist Series: Michael Andrew Law 2'
Paperback: 48 pages
ISBN-10: 1507581556
ISBN-13: 978-1507581551

Michael Andrew Law

(852) 6444-7550
info@michaelandrewlaw.com
www.michaelandrewlaw.com

Publications : Illustrated Books

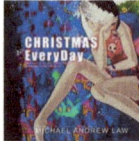

Christmas Everyday Book 1: Pale Hair Girls Christmas Series (Pale Hair Girls Christmas Everyday) (Volume 1)
ISBN-10: 1505453216
ISBN-13: 978-1505453218
Product Dimensions: 8.5 x 0.1 x 8.5 inches

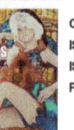

Christmas Everyday Book 2: Pale Hair Girls Christmas Series (Pale Hair Girls Christmas Everyday) (Volume 2)
ISBN-10: 1505467799
ISBN-13: 978-1505467796
Product Dimensions: 8.5 x 0.1 x 8.5 inches

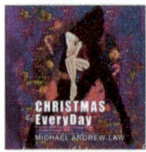

Christmas Everyday Book 3: Pale Hair Girls Christmas Series (Pale Hair Girls Christmas Everyday) (Volume 3)
ISBN-10: 1505468051
ISBN-13: 978-1505468052
Product Dimensions: 8.5 x 0.1 x 8.5 inches

Christmas Everyday Book 4: Pale Hair Girls Christmas Series (Pale Hair Girls Christmas Everyday) (Volume 4)
ISBN-10: 1505470749
ISBN-13: 978-1505470741
Product Dimensions: 8.5 x 0.1 x 8.5 inches

Christmas Everyday Book 5: Pale Hair Girls Christmas Series (Pale Hair Girls Christmas Everyday) (Volume 5)
ISBN-10: 1505470854
ISBN-13: 978-1505470857
Product Dimensions: 8.5 x 0.1 x 8.5 inches

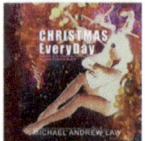

Christmas Everyday Book 6: Pale Hair Girls Christmas Series (Pale Hair Girls Christmas Everyday) (Volume 6)
ISBN-10: 150547115X
ISBN-13: 978-1505471151
Product Dimensions: 8.5 x 0.1 x 8.5 inches

Christmas Everyday: Special Edition (Pale Hair Girls Christmas Everyday) (Volume 7)
ISBN-10: 1505583926
ISBN-13: 978-1505583922
Product Dimensions: 8.5 x 0.3 x 8.5 inches

Michael Andrew Law

(852) 6444-7550
info@michaelandrewlaw.com
www.michaelandrewlaw.com

Selected Works for Art Events

iEgoism Exhibition at NatureArt ,Central District Hong Kong

iEgoism Exhibition In Photos (from left) : TV/ Movie stars Cherrie Kong ,Michael Andrew Law , Iva law ,Florence Lawman.

Michael Andrew Law exhibition at the Avenue of Stars, Hong Kong (星光大道).

Michael Andrew Law exhibition at the Avenue of Stars, Hong Kong (星光大道).

Art Related Events for Organic Beauty opening,

Art Talks at Credit Agricole CIB, Hong Kong Branch

Art Talks for The Rotary Club of Hong Kong At The Peninsula Hong Kong

Michael Andrew Law

(852) 6444-7550
info@michaelandrewlaw.com
www.michaelandrewlaw.com

Selected Works for Art Events

As Guest Art Tutor at Diocesan Boys' School

Working With Film Producer & Founder of Hollywood Film Institute Dov Simens.

Art Competition Award ceremony with Dr. Sarah Mary Liao , then-Secretary for the Environment of the Hong Kong Special Administrative Region .

Self Curated Exhibition with Art Collectors at Art Center ,2005.

Curated Art Events with The Swire Group (太古集團).

Curated Art Events with Hong Kong Stock Exchange (香港交易所).

Michael Andrew Law

(852) 6444-7550
info@michaelandrewlaw.com
www.michaelandrewlaw.com

Art Event with Young Men's Christian Association (YMCA).

Group Exhibition, Hong Kong Convention and Exhibition Centre.

iEgoism Exhibition

Exhibition, Elements, Hong Kong

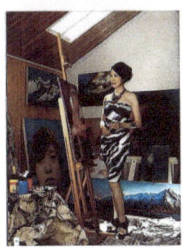

Oil Painting Shown in magazine :
壹周刊第1047期]第 20屆壹電視大獎 – 謝雪心

Michael Andrew Law

(852) 6444-7550
info@michaelandrewlaw.com
www.michaelandrewlaw.com

Selected Works for Art Events

Art Talk and Exhibition at Pui Shing Catholic Secondary School.

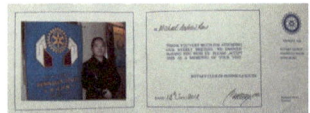

Art Talks and Charity Auction for The Rotary Club of Hong Kong At The Peninsula Hong Kong

Cardinal Zen Ze-kiun receives Michael Andrew Law at Ceremony. Comission portrait by Catholic Church of Hong Kong

Michael Andrew Law

(852) 6444-7550
info@michaelandrewlaw.com
www.michaelandrewlaw.com

The Pale Hair Universe Series

Medium : Traditional Oil Painting (With Acrylic Based) , Glitter , Gold Leaf .
About This Serie : Created Along with the First Series of painting of The Pale Hair Girls Original Series Paintings , Done with mixed media on canvas , with classical painting method.
Number of Paintings : 7 (As of 2015)
Availability : Limited Edition , Prints , Original Painting

Michael Andrew Law

(852) 6444-7550
info@michaelandrewlaw.com
www.michaelandrewlaw.com

Pale Hair Girls Original Series.

Medium : Traditional Oil Painting (With Acrylic Based) , Glitter , Gold Leaf .
About This Serie : First Series of painting of The entire Pale Hair Girls Universe ,
done with mixed media on canvas , with classical painting method.
Number of Paintings : 60 (As of 2015)
Availability : Limited Edition , Prints , Original Painting

Details

info@michaelandrewlaw.com
www.michaelandrewlaw.com

4'x 9' Multi-Panel Painting

30x20 ´ oil on canvas

S-P-R-I-N-G

info@michaelandrewlaw.com
www.michaelandrewlaw.com

© Michael Andrew Law™ 2014.All rights reserved

48x36 ″ oil on canvas

Nothing stops dreams

info@michaelandrewlaw.com
www.michaelandrewlaw.com

4'x 9' Multi-Panel Painting

info@michaelandrewlaw.com
www.michaelandrewlaw.com

© Michael Andrew Law™ 2014.All rights reserved

32x46 ˝ oil on canvas

Somewhere beyond my reach

info@michaelandrewlaw.com
www.michaelandrewlaw.com

36x48 ″ oil on canvas

Goodbye Future II

info@michaelandrewlaw.com
www.michaelandrewlaw.com

30x30 ″ oil on canvas

I only dreams cause I am Alive.

info@michaelandrewlaw.com
www.michaelandrewlaw.com

Michael Andrew Law

(852) 6444-7550
info@michaelandrewlaw.com
www.michaelandrewlaw.com

Pale Hair Girls : The New

Medium : Mixed Media Painting (oil and Acrylic) , Glitter , Gold Leaf .
About This Serie : Second Series of painting of The entire Pale Hair Girls Universe ,
done with mixed media on canvas , classical method crossover with contemporary Digital painting method.
Number of Paintings : 80 (As of 2015)
Availability : Limited Edition , Prints , Special Edition .

Michael Andrew Law

(852) 6444-7550
info@michaelandrewlaw.com
www.michaelandrewlaw.com

Pale Hair Girls : The New

Medium : Mixed Media Painting (oil and Acrylic) , Glitter , Gold Leaf .
About This Serie : Second Series of painting of The entire Pale Hair Girls Universe ,
done with mixed media on canvas , classical method crossover with contemporary Digital
painting method.
Number of Paintings : 80 (As of 2015)
Availability : Limited Edition , Prints , Special Edition .

Michael Andrew Law

(852) 6444-7550
info@michaelandrewlaw.com
www.michaelandrewlaw.com

Pale Hair Girls : Christmas Everyday

Medium : Mixed Media Painting (digital print with Acrylic) , Glitter , Gold Leaf .
About This Serie : Special Series illustrations of The Pale Hair Girls Universe ,
done with mixed media on canvas , classical method crossover with contemporary Digital
painting method.
Number of Paintings : 102 (As of 2015)
Availability : Limited Edition , Prints , Special Edition .

Forgive the guilty.

am I allowed to go Christmas shopping?

Peace on earth will come to stay, when we live Christmas every day

How all of our hopes Had come down to this child

Michael Andrew Law

(852) 6444-7550
info@michaelandrewlaw.com
www.michaelandrewlaw.com

Pale Hair Girls : iEgoism

Medium : Mixed Media Painting (oil and Acrylic) , Glitter , Gold Leaf .
About This Serie : Third Series of painting of The entire Pale Hair Girls Universe ,
done with mixed media on canvas , classical method crossover with contemporary painting method.
Number of Paintings : 960 (As of 2015)
Availability : Limited Edition , Prints , Special Edition .

Michael Andrew Law

(852) 6444-7550
info@michaelandrewlaw.com
www.michaelandrewlaw.com

Pale Hair Girls : iEgoism

Medium : Mixed Media Painting (oil and Acrylic) , Glitter , Gold Leaf .
About This Serie : Third Series of painting of The entire Pale Hair Girls Universe ,
done with mixed media on canvas , classical method crossover with contemporary painting method.
Number of Paintings : 960 (As of 2015)
Availability : Limited Edition , Prints , Special Edition .

有關藝術家的創作模式與批評

曾讀過很多文章是批評有很多藝術家變化太少，或將自己一次的成功無限複製；首先，當去理解一個藝術作品時，也必須同時去理解藝術家究竟是在解決甚麼問題。

多數藝術家最有創作力的時間也是在30歲前，那麼30歲前一個藝術家首要解決的問題就是-「生存下去」-既指事業上也指生命上吧。

然而，當你首要考慮的是生存時，便要開始理解他在做的藝術是怎麼「賣」的規則。

有關這個思路我在一部關於Jean Michel Basquiat 的傳記電影中有一段我人深刻的對白，年輕的Jean michel Basquiat 問他好朋友Benny Dalmau，怎樣才可作一位成功的藝術家[即要存活下來]，Benny Dalmau答道，"那你要發明一個畫風讓群眾記得你，然後一直堅持地畫，直至畫到悶得要死，仍畫下去，便會成功了。" 也許是個太幽默了一點的說法，卻道出了藝術家生存道上當中之精髓。[Jean michel basquiat其後以紐約塗鴉藝術家的身分開畫展獲得大眾認識，後來成為一位成功的1980年代表現主義藝術家，亦是今日當代畫拍賣價世界最貴之名列五大的一個藝術家。]

一個藝術家可以發明了一個自己的聲音，然後堅持創作，至成為真正藝術家[被買家認可]，然後再被人發現/品評，整個路程已很難吧，然而當達到所謂的成功時，第一的是，若

要保持成功 ， 最安全的便是保持既有模式吧 ， 讀者想真點:
藝術家這麼做要去到此境地已經先淘汰了一大羣兒戲份子而存
留認真者吧 ， 那些可以憑空叫得出名字的藝術家已經是萬中
無一 [例如:香港就只有馬榮成，黃玉郎 ，即使出名如「麥嘜」
的作畫家麥家碧已不是一般大眾能憑空叫得出名字的藝術家了
，若不計歌唱或表演界]， 若要他們跳出既有重覆的框框 ， 在
一個藝術家的立場來說當然非常危險 ，這麼做而失敗了的也多
得數不儘 ， 有些藝術家失敗了便立即停止並回到框框中以不
致 「損手爛腳」 ， 再稱那些轉型作品為失敗之作也就作罷 ；
當然有極少極少極少數可憑轉型而獲重大成功。
就如當代畫家艾軒 [艾未未同父異母之兄， 當代畫拍賣價世界
名列二十大最貴之一個中國藝術家。]那種演變自Andrew
Wyeth風格的維吾爾族少女油畫 ，從八十年代初至21世紀10年
代，幾乎是一摸一樣的---[先說清楚，我是個艾軒迷， 若我負
擔得來也想買一，兩幅來掛，只因為愛那種畫面的感覺。] 有
些藝術家的作品就是如此 ， 永遠是一個模式的 ，愛艾軒的畫
就是愛他那個模式 ， 問題是假設艾軒把那種風格的畫就只畫
有一張，再作其他不同風格 ， 你還會認識艾軒嗎 ？ 至少他未
必能憑一張混合Andrew Wyeth風格的畫便能生存下來 ， 在當
代美術界幾乎不可能 ，買家也不會對此產生認同感 。
所以這大慨解釋了藝術界的基本原則 ，首先是要發現一個成功
的模式後便倚靠那模式無限複製地存活下去[這已夠難了] ， 就
如像藤子不二雄的叮噹 多啦A夢 ， 好處是你必定認得是他的作

品 ，後隨者也只會被認為是藤子不二雄的隨者 ， 無限複製自己舊作的模式亦可使觀眾產生熟悉感 ，亦間接告訴觀眾「我是認真」的訊息 ， 才會稍為增加對這藝術家的安全感 ， 才再考慮投入感情或金錢吧。。

而經過了這麼多轉折 ， 再拿出勇氣或生存成本去再轉型本身不是易事 ， 亦不是義務吧 ， 老生常談的是沒有所謂一位藝術家或作品可以得世上每一位觀眾的認同或喜愛 ， 當解決了生存問題同時亦等於你已完成滿足了世上少部份的觀眾之所謂「藝術家的任務」了 ， 因為藝術家不是政客 ， 當一個藝術家的生存就可能只需100個或更少的人就夠了時 ， 其他關乎生存以外的意見或批評大多只流於理論或口舌之爭 ，亦多數對藝術家或作品本身也許沒有大多幫助罷 。

在此再說明我並非指藝術批評沒有其存在價值 ，只是指出藝術批評在藝術鬼腳圖上的位置 ；而就是該批評或理論是如何有建設性 ， 90%的藝術家在創作模式上首要考慮的還是生存 ，所謂理論多數仍是作品本身的副產品已 ，這個尤其在電影和影評中顯見 ，就如陳逸飛 [當代畫拍賣價世界最貴之名列十大的一個中國藝術家。]所言 ，一件作品要贏得到觀眾拍掌已夠難了 ，又同時要得到專家點頭則是罕有的例子 ，倒轉先有專家點頭而再因此[在此強調因此二字]得到觀眾拍掌就少見得多了。

即使在博物館看過的至當代所謂的大師 ， 由17世紀的Rem-brandt 的畫布數至吳宇森的銀幕 ， 無不是先解決了生存的問題 ，再去想自己在歷史的位置罷 [當然最後他們也成了存活下來赢家]。

Michael Andrew Law at Work.

Michael Andrew Law fusing digital and classical painting with west and East creative philosophy , to produce an extremely original artistic language and content that bridged west and east ,classical and modern medium , at the same time clearly tells the stories of his own generation. Combining digital creative materials and classical painting techniques with effusive yet knowing and precise focused , his paintings maintain a powerful tension between opposing aesthetic forces—expression and knowledge, control and spontaneity, savagery and wit, urbanity and primitivism—while providing satiric commentary on the oppressive realities of the predicament of Generation Internet, homegrown hongkonger's local-culture vesus Traditional Chinese culture, and The Hong Kong's post-handover history.

In his dynamically designed compositions, gracefully detailed figures and innocent faces are incise against fields that juxtaposed with portraits, chinese calligraphy, and sometimes cgi. The Pale Hair Girls Series (2006 - 2013) depicts realistic cold, icy-like young female figures surrounded by abstract and expressively painted forms and shapes revealing images of Pop culture, Historial figures, and Hong Kong landmarks.

Michael Andrew Law draws inspiration from Old Master's works such as Caravaggio , Ruben , Rembrandt , all the way to the Modern Art Superstars such as Warhol , Lichtenstein , Richter , De Kooning , Bacon , Wool and Prince . The Pale Hair Girls series mainly inspired by the painting works of French academic painter and traditionalist William-Adolphe Bouguereau and the Late Great YiFei Chen's characteristic "Romantic Realism" paintings.

In a reversal of standard East-West aesthetics, Law re-interprets Old Master's sophisticated imagery combine classical and digital materials—which resonate with Digital Vector Designs and Paintings—with fine strokes of oil paint multi-layered with paint film.In his interpretation of Leonardo Da Vinci's iconic Mona Lisa's smile (1517)—an iconic image that has been endlessly disseminated and reproduced—Law painted over the symbolism of the portrait Mona Lisa with his young wife , intent on rendering the figure in contemporary fashion with the iconic image as background .

"The Humanity triptych" depicts New Generation HongKongers in a Ruined Hong Kong city , awaiting their unknown fate of a new beginning. This painting series explores one of the central paradox of his art—between romance and derision , his romantic magnanimity as an artist and his pessimistic perspective on the predicament of Generation Y Hongkongers. Here, this paradox is symbolized by the stark contrast of icy cold young female and disturbing representations of the armageddon-like of images. Whether portrayed as single "chinese calligraphy " or in triptych composition and classical paintwork that combine both expressive and traditional painting techniques with the digital vector , the beauties and the human figures stand as eternal motifs in the history of art and also in popular culture. Both oppositional and parallel, they are reminders of the fragile vibrancy of life and the impitoyable passing of time.

A references between different cultural refrence (high/pop, classical/contemporary, east/west), Michael Andrew Law has stated that an artist should be someone who understood how to hybrid between different worlds and go ahead makes an effort to knowing them. With his distinctive "iEgoism" philosophy , which employs highly refined academic painting techniques to depict a mixture of abstract expressionism within a representational pop culture images. These techniques parallel to the themes of romance and predicament of this generation , he recollects and revitalizes narratives of irony and introspection.

Michael Andrew Law was born in 1982 in British Hong Kong , studied fine art with american artist Daniel Anderson and with artist graduatee of China Central Academy of Fine Arts Sam Zeng from 2003 - 2006 . He co-founded the Hong Kong Art Studio Nature Art Workshop in 2008. In addition to the production and marketing of Michael Andrew Law's art and related work, Nature Art functions as a supportive environment for the
fostering of emerging Hong Konger artists. Law is also a curator. In 2013, he organized an exhibition of contemporary art titled "iEgoism ," which served as a commentaries of contemporary HongKong Gen Y pop culture ;These Theroy also published in the book : "iEgoism" in 2014.

Michael Andrew Law currently works and lives in Hong Kong.

For further information please contact the studio at info@michaelandrewlaw.com or at +852.6444.7550. All images are subject to copyright. Artist/Studio/Gallery's approval must be granted prior to reproduction.

2010 Avenue of Stars, Hong Kong

Exhibition :

2013 DeTour Matters 2013 Satellite Events at NatureArt Gallery
2013 December to Remember , One man show at NatureArt Gallery Central District, Hong Kong.
2012 Solo Show , Park Central tseung kwan O ,Hong Kong
2011 Art Walk Group Showing , Discovery Bay ,Hong Kong
2011 HK Gold Coast (Book signing exhibition)
2009 Solo Painting Exhibition The Avenue of Stars
Group Exhibition of Daniel Anderson workshop Classical Realism class of 2008 at Manhattan,NY
2007 Guest and ExhibitionThe Peak Galleria Hong Kong
2007 Invited workshop exhibition, Elements, Hong Kong
Group Exhibition of Classical Realism class of 2007 at Manhattan,NY
2006 Collection by Cardinal Zen Ze-kiun and exhibited at Catholic Church of Hong Kong.
2004 - 2007, Hong Kong Young Artist Group Exhibition, Hong Kong Central Library.
Group Exhibition of Classical Realism class of 2006 at East Village, Manhattan,NY
2005 Illustration original exhibition for Kung Kao Po
2004 Group Exhibition, Hong Kong Convention and Exhibition Centre.
2004 Group Exhibition, Wanchai Tower
2003 Group Exhibition, Hong Kong Convention and Exhibition Centre.
2003 Winner of I luv Hong Kong Painting Competition, exhibition at The Landmark (Hong Kong).
2002 The Holy story Picture Book illustrated picture original exhibition ,sai wan ho civic centre.

SELECTED COLLECTIONS :

Cardinal of the Catholic Church Joseph Zen Ze-kiun
Organic Beauty Inc
Agriculture, Fisheries and Conservation Department
Ms.Ho Wei Ying
Ms. Annie Yu
Daniel Anderson
MR.Tsang Yan Sam

PUBLICATIONS :

Fisheye magazine , featured artist interview , November 2002
Kung Kao Po , interview , June 2006
Art of Rock Realism , 2008
The Art of Michael Andrew Law , 2010
December to Remember One man Show Art Book , 2013
iEgoism , 2015

Solo Shows 2010 - 2013

I really appreciate your purchase of this Painting

Collection Book , I hope you enjoy reading them as

much as I enjoyed painting them!

May God bless your home with peace, joy and love.

From Michael Andrew Law.

Find Me Online.

Michael Andrew Law   Q

www.ingramcontent.com/pod-product-compliance
Lightning Source LLC
Chambersburg PA
CBHW040749200526
45159CB00025B/1813